ISLE OF H
TRAVEL GUIDE 2023

Discover the Untamed Beauty of the Isle of Harris: Your Ultimate Travel Guide"

By

John Emmanuel

Table of contents

Tourist Information Center

Welcome

Welcome to the Isle of Harris, a gem in Scotland's Outer Hebrides' rugged beauty! Prepare to be captivated by this idyllic island's pristine white sand beaches, turquoise waters, and breathtaking landscapes as soon as you arrive.

You will come across a land with a long history and ancient customs as you travel through the moorlands and rolling hills. Gaelic culture is alive and well on the Isle of Harris, where music, language, and craftsmanship thrive. Engage in conversation with the friendly locals whose tales will leave an indelible mark on your soul as you take in the mellow tones of traditional music that fill the air.

Explore the world-famous Harris Tweed, a fabric made by skilled artisans using traditional methods. Witness the inventiveness that goes into creating these vibrant colors and intricate patterns, and you might take home a piece of this genuine heritage as a prized keepsake.

The Isle of Harris is a haven of natural wonders for nature lovers. Take in the revitalizing sea breeze as you stroll along the pristine shorelines where the waves gently caress the shores. You will be in awe as you marvel at the dramatic cliffs that stand majestically against the Atlantic Ocean's crashing waves.

Take a trip to Harris's surrounding uninhabited islands, where seabird colonies and marine life thrive without being disturbed. White-tailed eagles' graceful flight, playful seals' basking on rocky outcrops, and, if you're lucky, the majestic whales that inhabit these waters can all be observed.

Take in the island's culinary delights and the best seafood from the surrounding waters as you indulge your taste buds. Get ready for a culinary experience that highlights the island's natural bounty, from succulent langoustines to delicate smoked salmon.

Be prepared to take in some of the most mesmerizing sunsets you'll ever see as the day turns into night. You'll understand why those who have had the opportunity to visit the Isle of

Harris hold a special place in their hearts when you see the sky filled with gold, orange, and pink tones.

Thus, welcome to the Isle of Harris, where time stops, and the soul of the island will embrace you with great enthusiasm. Plan to leave on a wonderful excursion loaded up with stunning scenes, social fortunes, and remarkable minutes. I hope that your time on this magical island will be truly extraordinary.

Introduction

Welcome to the enchanting Isle of Harris, a hidden gem in the stunning Scottish Hebrides archipelago. With its rough shores, unblemished sandy sea shores, and sensational scenes, Harris offers an unprecedented break into immaculate normal excellence. This spellbinding island, situated off the northwest shoreline of Scotland, is famous for its dynamic Gaelic culture, antiquated history, and flourishing distinctive practices.

The striking scenery of Harris will immediately captivate you as soon as you step foot on the island. Magnificent mountains covered in fog rule the skyline, while flowing cascades tumble down steep precipices into completely clear lochs. The pure white sands contrast sharply with the deep azure waters of the Atlantic Ocean, making the coastline a natural artist's masterpiece.

The world-renowned Harris Tweed, a handwoven fabric that has come to represent quality, craftsmanship, and timeless style, is one of the island's most recognizable features. Visit the skilled weavers in their remote cottages to immerse yourself in the age-old art of weaving. There, they meticulously use vibrant natural dyes to create intricate designs.

Harris is also a haven for nature lovers thanks to its abundance of wildlife. Take a boat tour to see the playful dolphins and whales that inhabit these waters, watch soaring sea eagles soar through the sky, and look for lazy seals on remote beaches.

The island's ancient landmarks and archaeological sites offer a fascinating look back at the past for history buffs. Visit the historic St. Clement's Church, a picturesque medieval church with a view of the rugged coastline, or the enigmatic standing stones of Callanish, a prehistoric stone circle that has baffled archaeologists for centuries.

Harris provides the ideal retreat for recuperation and rejuvenation. Relax on the island's pristine beaches, like the well-known Luskentyre, with their tranquil turquoise waters and golden sands. Enjoy the serenity of nature's embrace and the clean sea air by taking leisurely strolls along coastal paths.

Enjoy the island's renowned culinary delights as the day winds down and take advantage of the warm welcome offered by the locals. Enjoy a fine selection of whiskies from nearby distilleries alongside succulent Harris lobsters and locally caught scallops.

The Isle of Harris is a captivating journey into a world of wild beauty, ancient customs, and genuine community, whether you're looking for adventure, cultural discovery, or a peaceful escape. Allow the enchantment of Harris to surround you and prepare to be captivated by the island's rugged charm.

About Isle Of Harris island

The Outer Hebrides, a group of islands off the west coast of mainland Scotland, include the island of Harris.

It is well-known for its breathtaking natural beauty, which includes dramatic landscapes with rocky mountains, golden sand beaches, and clear turquoise waters.

The Isle of Harris is renowned for its Harris Tweed, a handwoven texture that is created on the island. Harris Tweed is well-known all over the world for its durability and unique patterns.

The Gaelic language is still spoken by a significant number of island residents, and the island has a rich Gaelic heritage.

Tarbert is the main settlement on the Isle of Harris. It is a transportation hub and has accommodations, shops, and other amenities.

On the west coast of Harris, Luskentyre Beach is frequently ranked among the world's most stunning beaches. Visitors come from far and wide to enjoy its turquoise waters and white sands.

Seals, otters, golden eagles, and red deer are just some of the many species of wildlife that call the Isle of Harris their home. Diverse marine life can also be found in the waters around.

There are opportunities for water sports, hiking, fishing, bird watching, and other outdoor activities on the island. The island's natural wonders can be explored on a variety of trails and paths.

St. Forebearing's Congregation in Rodel is a memorable site on the Isle of Harris. It is a medieval church with stunning views of the Sound of Harris and intricate stone carvings.

A land bridge connects the Isle of Harris and the Isle of Lewis, allowing visitors to easily explore both islands. Lewis and Harris is a common name for the combined area.

Tourism, fishing, and agriculture make up the majority of the island's revenue. The island's rich cultural heritage can be explored, local seafood can be enjoyed, and traditional crofting communities can be visited.

Due to its unspoiled landscapes and unusual lighting, the Isle of Harris is a popular destination for artists, photographers, and nature enthusiasts.

On the nearby Isle of Lewis are the well-known standing stones of Callanish, a Neolithic stone circle. They are a must-see attraction for visitors to the region and a significant archaeological site.

The Isle of Harris Gin is made at the Tarbert-based Isle of Harris Distillery. It is known for its distinctive flavor and botanicals that are foraged locally.

The Isle of Harris has been highlighted in a few movies and Television programs, including the famous BBC series "Castaway" and the film "The Rocket Post."

These details reveal the Isle of Harris singular beauty and cultural significance, making it a charming destination for travelers looking for an unforgettable experience.

Geography and Climate

The Outer Hebrides, an archipelago off the west coast of mainland Scotland, contain the stunning Isle of Harris. It is a part of the larger Isle of Harris and Lewis landmass, which is connected by a narrow isthmus. Lewis lives in the north of the island, while Harris lives in the south.

The rugged and dramatic landscape of the Isle of Harris is what sets it apart geographically. It includes a different scope of landscape, including rough slopes, heather-covered moorlands, lovely white sandy sea shores, and beautiful fjord-like ocean lochs. The island is encircled by the sky blue waters of the Atlantic

Sea, making an amazing waterfront landscape. The most popular ocean side on Harris is Luskentyre, eminent for its immaculate white sands and completely clear turquoise waters.

The environment of the Isle of Harris is a delegated sea, intensely impacted by the encompassing sea. Throughout the year, the weather can fluctuate between sunny skies, clouds, wind, and rain. Summers are gentle and lovely, with normal temperatures going from 12°C to 18°C (54°F to 64°F). The best time to enjoy outdoor activities and see the island's natural beauty is now.

The average winter temperature is 5°C, with occasional frost and snowfall on higher ground, and it ranges from 41°F to 48°F. The island encounters regular precipitation, particularly during the harvest time and cold weather months. This precipitation adds to the rich vegetation that covers the scene, including heather, grasses, and greeneries.

The Isle of Harris is known for major areas of strength for its, which can make a feeling of ferocity and add to the sensational climate. The island's terrain is shaped by these winds, which also contribute to its unique character. Windsurfers and kite surfers who want to take advantage of the challenging conditions on the island gravitate to them.

The Isle of Harris is a haven for nature lovers, photographers, and those seeking a tranquil retreat due to its climate and geography. It is an unforgettable destination for visitors from all over the world due to its unspoiled beauty, which is combined with the one-of-a-kind combination of rugged mountains, pristine beaches, and weather that changes constantly.

Brief History

The Outer Hebrides, an archipelago off the west coast of Scotland, include the picturesque Isle of Harris. The Isle of Harris has a fascinating history that spans centuries and is full of natural beauty as well as rich history. Let's travel through its past together:

A long time ago:

On the Isle of Harris, the earliest evidence of human settlement dates back thousands of years. Archeological proof proposes that a Neolithic and Bronze Age people group occupied the island, abandoning ancient rarities, for example, standing stones and internment locales.

Viking Impact:

The Isle of Harris was a part of the Norse Kingdom of the Isles during the Viking Age, which lasted from the 8th century to the 13th century. The island was settled by Norwegian Vikings who brought their language, culture, and way of life with them. The impact of the Vikings can in any case be seen today in the names of many puts on the island.

The Clans of MacLeod and MacNeil:

In the thirteenth 100 years, the Family MacLeod, dropped from Norse progenitors, oversaw the Isle of Harris. They laid out their fortification at Dunvegan Palace on the adjoining Isle of Skye, however applied impact over Harris and the encompassing islands. The MacLeods administered the region for a very long time.

However, parts of the Isle of Harris were also ruled by another prominent clan, Clan MacNeil. The MacNeils, initially from Barra, asserted responsibility for the southern piece of the island, with their seat at the now-demolished Rodel Church.

Crofting and the Clearances:

The Highlands and islands of Scotland underwent significant social and economic transformations in the 19th century. On the Isle of Harris, crofting, or small-scale subsistence farming, became common. The crofters lived in little, scattered networks and worked the land for their job.

However, during the Highland Clearances, a lot of landlords tried to clear land from tenant farmers and use it for sheep farming, which was more profitable. Many crofters were evicted from their ancestral lands as a result, putting them through a great deal of hardship and forcing many to emigrate to other parts of Scotland or overseas.

Tweed Harris:

One of the most famous parts of the Isle of Harris is its relationship with Harris Tweed. The island's weaving industry flourished in the middle of the 19th century, with locals producing tweed fabric from wool sourced locally. The distinctive Harris Tweed became synonymous with the island and gained worldwide popularity due to its durability and vibrant colors.

Present day Times:

The Isle of Harris saw improvements in its infrastructure during the 20th century, including the construction of roads and the introduction of electricity. These advancements carried expanded availability to the island and worked on the personal satisfaction for its occupants.

Today, visitors from all over the world flock to the Isle of Harris to take in its stunning landscapes, pristine beaches, and distinctive cultural heritage. The island's natural beauty, traditional crafts, and resilience continue to attract admiration.

This is a concise outline of the historical backdrop of the Isle of Harris, catching a portion of its huge achievements and impacts. A rich tapestry of tales that have shaped the island's identity and contributed to its current status as a beloved destination can be discovered by delving deeper into its past.

Chapter One

Best Time to Visit

The Isle of Harris, situated in the External Hebrides of Scotland, offers stunning scenes, perfect sea shores, and a rich social legacy. Picking the best opportunity to visit the Isle of Harris relies upon your inclinations and what you desire to encounter during your excursion. Here are a few elements to consider while arranging your visit:

Weather: The Isle of Harris' maritime location has an impact on the weather, which can change quickly. From June to August, the summer months typically have the highest average temperatures, ranging from 14°C to 17°C (57°F to 63°F). However, rain showers are possible at any time of the year, so it's always a good idea to bring clothing that can be adjusted to the changing conditions.

Wildlife: Assuming you're keen on untamed life detecting, the best chance to visit the Isle of Harris is throughout the spring and mid year months. This is when seabird provinces, like puffins and razorbills, are settling on the bluffs, and you could likewise detect seals and dolphins along the coast. Bring your binoculars because the island is famous for its birdwatching opportunities!

Beaches: The Isle of Harris is famous for its staggering sea shores, highlighting flawless white sands and turquoise waters. The best weather for beach activities like sunbathing, swimming, and picnicking is in the summer. Be prepared, however, for a refreshing dip because the sea temperature can be quite chilly even during the warmer months!

Scene and Photography: The tough and emotional scene of the Isle of Harris is a picture taker's fantasy. The heather turns purple during the autumn months, from September to November, and the hillsides become golden with bracken. Especially at sunrise and sunset, the soft light of spring and summer can also produce breathtaking scenes.

Groups and Convenience: The Isle of Harris is a popular vacation spot, and during the summer's busiest times, it can draw a sizable crowd. Consider visiting during the shoulder seasons, such as late spring (May) or early autumn (September), if you prefer a quieter experience with fewer visitors. Throughout the year, there are a variety of lodging options, such as hotels, bed and breakfasts, and cottages with self-catering facilities. During peak times, however, it is recommended to book in advance.

The best time to visit the Isle of Harris ultimately depends on your interests and preferences. Whether you're looking for outside experiences, natural life experiences, tranquil strolls, or just an opportunity to drench yourself in the island's one of a kind culture, Harris offers something exceptional all year.

Entry Requirements

There are a few things you need to know in order to enter the Isle of Harris, which is part of the Outer Hebrides in Scotland. Here are a few basic principles:

Documents for Travel: To enter the United Kingdom and travel within Scotland, make sure you have the necessary travel documents. For visitors from outside the United States, this usually includes a valid passport. Check with the applicable experts for the most exceptional necessities.

Requirements for a Visa: To enter the United Kingdom, you may need a visa, depending on your nationality. Affirm whether you really want a visa ahead of time and apply in a like manner.

Restrictions for COVID-19: There may be specific entry requirements and travel restrictions imposed as a result of the ongoing COVID-19 pandemic. It is essential to check the most recent guidelines from official government sources, such as the websites of the UK and

Scottish governments, as these can change rapidly. This includes any requirements for testing or quarantine.

Transport: Examine the available modes of transportation to get to the Isle of Harris. You might have to design your process via air or ocean, as the island is situated off the west shoreline of Scotland. Guarantee you have affirmed appointments for your favored method of transport.

Accommodation: Orchestrate your convenience ahead of time, as accessibility on the island might change relying upon the season. Hotels, guesthouses, cottages with self-catering options, and campsites are just some of the options available in Harris. To guarantee your preferred option, make sure to book your lodging in advance.

Itinerary: Plan your schedule and exercises on the Isle of Harris, considering the span of your visit and the attractions you wish to visit. The island is known for its staggering scenes, delightful sea shores, and rich social legacy.

Outdoor gear: On the Isle of Harris, the weather can change depending on the time of year. To ensure your comfort and safety during your visit, bring appropriate clothing and outdoor gear. It is consistently prudent to have waterproof and comfortable dress, no matter what the season.

Cultural and natural respect: The Isle of Harris is renowned for its vibrant Gaelic culture and pristine natural beauty. Respect the environment by adhering to local customs and traditions and adhering to the Leave No Trace principles.

Keep in mind that requirements and restrictions may change, so double-check the most recent information and guidelines closer to your travel date.

Visa Requirements

The Isle of Harris is essential for the External Hebrides, which is a gathering of islands in

Scotland. Therefore, depending on your nationality and the UK's immigration policies, you will need a visa to visit the Isle of Harris. Please keep in mind that immigration policies can change, so you should always check with the appropriate authorities or the British embassy or consulate closest to you for the most recent information. Some general information is as follows:

Switzerland, the European Union (EU), and the European Economic Area (EEA): The United Kingdom, including Scotland, is open to citizens of Switzerland, the European Economic Area, and the European Union (EEA) at the time of my knowledge cutoff. Notwithstanding, this might have changed because of the UK's withdrawal from the EU. Checking the most recent requirements is fundamental.

Non-EU/EEA Residents: You may need a visa to enter the United Kingdom, including the Isle of Harris, if you are not a citizen of Switzerland, the European Economic Area, or the European Union. The particular visa prerequisites will rely upon your ethnicity, reason for visit, and span of stay. Before traveling, you would need to apply for the appropriate visa.

Visa for Travel: A Standard Visitor Visa may be required if you intend to travel to the Isle of Harris for business purposes. This visa permits you to remain in the UK for as long as a half year for the travel industry, seeing family or companions, or taking part in specific business-related exercises.

Visa for Work or Study: You will likely need to apply for the appropriate visa category, such as a Tier 2 (General) visa for work or a Tier 4 visa for study, if you intend to work or study on the Isle of Harris. There are particular requirements and procedures for applying for these visas.

It's urgent to note that the Isle of Harris is important for the Unified Realm, and similar migration rules and visa necessities apply with respect to different pieces of the country. For the most up-to-date and accurate information on the requirements for obtaining a visa to visit the Isle of Harris, you should check the Home Office website or the British embassy or consulate closest to you.

Getting There

You'll need to carefully plan your journey in order to reach the stunning Isle of Harris, which is in Scotland's Outer Hebrides. While it very well might be a remote and detached objective, arriving at the Isle of Harris is most certainly worth the work. Here is a manual for assist you with exploring your direction to this lovely island:

Picking Your Method of Transportation: The Isle of Harris can be reached primarily in two ways: by plane or ferry.

a. **Via Air:** The closest air terminal to the Isle of Harris is Stornoway Air terminal (SYY) on the adjoining Isle of Lewis. From major Scottish cities like Glasgow, Edinburgh, or Inverness, you can fly to Stornoway Airport. From Stornoway, you can either employ a vehicle or take public transport to Tarbert, the principal town on the Isle of Harris. By road, the trip from Stornoway to Tarbert takes between 1.5 and 2 hours.

b. **By boat**: CalMac Ships works normal ship administrations to the Isle of Harris from Ullapool on the Scottish central area. The ship venture requires close to 2 hours and 30 minutes, and you can bring your vehicle along. To guarantee your spot, it is best to reserve your ferry tickets in advance, particularly during peak tourist seasons.

Arriving on Harris Island: When you show up at Tarbert, the principal port and managerial focus of the island, you'll wind up in the core of the Isle of Harris. Accommodations, restaurants, and shops are just a few of the many amenities in Tarbert. In the event that you're not remaining in Tarbert, you can continue to your picked convenience, whether it's an inn, guesthouse, or self-providing food cabin.

Exploring Harris Island: With its stunning scenes, unblemished sea shores, and rough shoreline, the Isle of Harris brings a lot to the table. Here are a few features to investigate:

a. Beach at Luskentyre: Quite possibly the most beautiful ocean side in Scotland, Luskentyre Ocean side flaunts turquoise waters, far reaching white sands, and amazing mountain vistas. Photographers and beach lovers should definitely go there.

Harris Tweed, b: The traditional tweed fabric that Harris produces is well-known. You can learn about the history, production, and authentic Harris Tweed products by going to the Harris Tweed Shop in Tarbert or the Harris Tweed Gallery in Drinishader.

c. Isle of Harris Refinery: The Isle of Harris Distillery is a must-see for anyone who enjoys whisky. You can take a directed visit to find out about the whisky-production cycle and test a portion of their acclaimed single malt.

d. Scalpay: Associated with the Isle of Harris by a scaffold, the little island of Scalpay offers delightful beach front strolls and perspectives on the encompassing region. It's a tranquil retreat that's worth a visit.

How to Get Around Harris Island: Having your own vehicle is the most helpful method for investigating the Isle of Harris. You can either lease a vehicle from Stornoway or welcome your vehicle on the ship from Ullapool. On the other hand, in the event that you don't really want to drive, there is a restricted transport administration on the island, despite the fact that checking the timetable in advance is fundamental.

Arranging Your Visit: There are a variety of places to stay on the Isle of Harris, such as hotels, guesthouses, bed and breakfasts, and cottages with their own kitchens. It's fitting to book your convenience ahead of time, especially throughout the late spring months when the island encounters a deluge of vacationers.

Before you go on a trip, check the most recent travel guidelines and ferry times, as they may change from time to time.

Transportation

On the Isle of Harris, situated in the External Hebrides of Scotland, there are a few methods for transportation accessible to investigate the island and its environmental factors. Here are a few well known methods of transportation on the Isle of Harris:

Vehicle Rental: Leasing a vehicle is a famous choice for investigating the Isle of Harris. There are vehicle rental organizations accessible on the island, and having a vehicle gives you the opportunity to go at your own speed and access distant regions. It's essential to take note of that most rental organizations require a legitimate driver's permit and may have age limitations.

Cycling: Cycling is a phenomenal method for investigating the Isle of Harris, offering a slower speed that permits you to see the value in the island's shocking scencs and shore. You can bring your own bicycle or lease one from nearby rental shops.

Transport: The Isle of Harris is served by a nearby transport administration, worked by the organization known as the Hebridean Vehicle Organization. The transport courses cover different pieces of the island and give a helpful method for transportation for the two local people and guests. In any case, it's essential to check the transport plan in advance, as administrations might be restricted, particularly during ends of the week and occasions.

Taxi: Cabs are accessible on the Isle of Harris, offering a more customized transportation choice. You can enlist a taxi to take you to explicit objections or for directed visits around the island. It's fitting to book a taxi ahead of time, particularly during the pinnacle traveler season.

Strolling: The Isle of Harris flaunts stunning scenes, and numerous guests decide to investigate the island by walking. There are various strolling trails and ways that permit you to find the island's normal magnificence, including the popular Harris Walkway. Make a point to wear suitable footwear and convey essential arrangements while setting out on longer climbs.

Boat Visits: To investigate the waterfront regions and close by islands, you can decide on boat visits. Different visit administrators offer excursions to the dazzling sea shores, ocean stacks, and marine natural life rich regions encompassing the Isle of Harris. These visits frequently withdraw from explicit focuses on the island and give a one of a kind viewpoint of the area.

Make sure to design your transportation ahead of time, particularly during top vacationer seasons, and check for any neighborhood guidelines or rules with respect to transportation on the Isle of Harris.

Accommodations

In the Outer Hebrides of Scotland, the Isle of Harris has a variety of lodging options to suit a variety of preferences and budgets. Whether you're looking for a comfortable guesthouse, a conventional quaint little inn, a self-cooking cabin, or a lavish inn, you'll track down reasonable choices on this beautiful island. Here are a few sorts of facilities you can consider while visiting the Isle of Harris:

Hotels: On the Isle of Harris, there are a number of hotels with a variety of amenities and comfortable rooms. You can choose from smaller hotels to larger establishments based on your preferences. A few inns offer shocking ocean views and are many times situated close to famous attractions or beautiful sea shores.

B&Bs and guesthouses: Guesthouses and overnight boarding house foundations are well known decisions for those looking for a more private and personal experience. Cozy rooms, hearty Scottish breakfasts, and a welcoming atmosphere are frequently found in these lodgings. Numerous guesthouses and B&Bs are situated in beguiling towns, permitting you to drench yourself in the nearby local area.

Self-Providing food Bungalows: Self-catering cottages are an excellent option if you value independence and the freedom to prepare your own meals. These lodgings come in a variety of styles, from traditional thatched cottages to contemporary vacation homes that frequently have all of the necessary amenities. Self-cooking choices are especially reasonable for families or gatherings searching for open facilities.

Camping areas and Train Parks: For open air lovers, the Isle of Harris offers campgrounds and parade parks where you can set up a shelter or park your troop or RV. These destinations frequently give fundamental offices like showers, latrines, and electric snare ups, permitting you to partake in the island's regular excellence and rough scenes.

Unique Places to Stay: You might want to think about looking into different lodging options if you want an experience that is more original and memorable. Converted crofts, which are traditional Scottish cottages, eco-friendly lodges, and even glamping sites, which provide luxurious camping experiences with comfortable amenities, are some options.

It is essential to reserve lodging well in advance when planning your stay on the Isle of Harris, particularly during peak tourist seasons. Take into consideration how close your chosen lodging is to the things you want to do and see on the island. The Isle of Harris has a wide variety of accommodations to meet the needs of every traveler, whether you're looking for peace and quiet, breathtaking landscapes, or the chance to learn about the rich culture of the Outer Hebrides.

Packing Essentials

While getting ready for a little while to the lovely Isle of Harris, situated in the External Hebrides of Scotland, it's crucial to pack properly to guarantee you have an agreeable and charming experience. The following are some things you should pack:

Clothing: Layers are essential because the Isle of Harris's weather can be unpredictable. Incorporate waterproof and windproof outerwear, for example, a decent quality downpour coat and tough strolling boots. For cooler days, bring comfortable trousers or jeans, long-sleeved shirts, and a sweater. If you intend to take a dip in the stunning beaches of the island, don't forget to bring some swimwear.

Outside Stuff: Pack some essentials for the outdoors if you want to see the island's beautiful landscapes. A sturdy water bottle, a hat, sunglasses, sunscreen, insect repellent, and a backpack are all examples of these. Furthermore, on the off chance that you appreciate climbing, bring a guide and a compass or a GPS gadget to explore the paths.

Camera: Be sure to take pictures of the stunning wildlife and landscapes on the Isle of Harris because of its stunning natural beauty. Carry a camera or a cell phone with a decent camera to report your experiences. Spare batteries, memory cards, and a versatile charger can likewise prove to be useful.

Adapters for Travel: Type G outlets are used in the United Kingdom, including the Isle of Harris. Be sure to bring the necessary travel adapters to charge your electronic devices if you are traveling from a country with different plug types.

Individual Consideration Things: Include a toothbrush, toothpaste, shampoo, conditioner, and any other necessary personal care items in your packing list. Even though there are shops on the island, you should bring only the essentials, especially if you have particular preferences.

Medications: Make sure you have enough medication for the duration of your trip if you take any medications. Convey them in their unique bundling, alongside any essential remedies or clinical archives. It's likewise prudent to bring a fundamental medical aid unit for minor wounds or infirmities.

Money and Cards: Even though the island has ATMs and card payment facilities, it is best to bring some cash with you, especially if you want to visit more remote areas where card acceptance may be limited.

Manuals and Guides: There are a lot of things to do and see on the Isle of Harris. Bringing maps or a guidebook can help you get around the island and find its treasures.

Entertainment: On the off chance that you appreciate pursuing or enjoying a specific side interest, bring along a book, a magazine, or some other type of diversion to appreciate during personal time or in the event of harsh weather conditions.

Tidbits and Water: Even though there are places to eat on the Isle of Harris, you should bring snacks and bottled water with you if you plan to spend a lot of time outside or explore remote areas.

Make sure to appropriately look at the neighborhood weather conditions before your excursion and pack. Pressing shrewdly guarantees you're ready for different exercises and conditions on the Isle of Harris, permitting you to take full advantage of your visit to this beautiful island heaven.

Chapter Two

Historical and Cultural sites

The island is home to a number of historical and cultural sites that provide a glimpse into its fascinating past and are well-known for their rugged landscapes, pristine beaches, and extensive cultural heritage. On the Isle of Harris, you can visit the following notable locations:

St. Forebearing's Congregation, Rodel: St. Forgiving Congregation is a lovely middle age church situated in the town of Rodel. It is one of Scotland's finest examples of pre-Reformation churches, built in the late 15th century. The congregation highlights perplexing carvings, a noteworthy internment path, and a striking burial chamber accepted to have a place with

Alexander MacLeod, a sixteenth century clan leader.

Callanish's Standing Stones: The Callanish Standing Stones are a remarkable prehistoric monument that can be reached easily from Harris, despite being on the Isle of Lewis that is adjacent. These rows and circles of stone are thought to have been used as an astronomical observatory or for a ceremony around 3000 BC. The location provides breathtaking views of the surrounding landscape and a mystical atmosphere.

Gearrannan's Blackhouse Village: Gearrannan is a reestablished blackhouse town that gives a brief look into customary island life. The Outer Hebrides used to be home to a lot of traditional stone and turf-roofed blackhouses. The island's crofting history can be explored, traditional crafts like weaving and peat cutting can be learned about, and the preserved blackhouses can be explored.

Seallam! Center for Guests: Located in Seallam, Northton! The Visitor Centre is a cultural hub that highlights the Isle of Harris's history, language, and customs. Exhibitions on crofting, the Harris Tweed industry, and the Gaelic language are on display at the center. It also has live demonstrations, educational programs, and a gift shop where you can buy locally made goods and crafts.

Beach Luskentyre: While not a verifiable site in the customary sense, Luskentyre Ocean side is a must-visit objective on the Isle of Harris. It is frequently referred to as one of the world's most stunning beaches due to its pristine white sands, turquoise waters, and dramatic mountain backdrop. The beach gives you a chance to see the island's natural beauty firsthand and offers breathtaking panoramic views.

On the Isle of Harris, you can visit a wide range of cultural and historical landmarks. Investigating these areas won't just give a more profound comprehension of the island's past yet additionally permit you to see the value in its normal miracles and the novel lifestyle of its occupants

Local crafts and Art works

The stunning natural landscapes and extensive cultural heritage of the Isle of Harris in Scotland's Outer Hebrides are well-known. The island's talented artisans' handiwork and crafts are one aspect of its vibrant culture. Here are a few outstanding instances of neighborhood specialties and workmanship on the Isle of Harris:

Tweed Harris: The textile known as Harris Tweed has come to be associated with the Isle of Harris. It is a handwoven texture produced using unadulterated virgin fleece, colored and turned on the island. Unique tweed patterns and designs are created by the weavers using traditional methods that have been passed down through the generations. Products such as home furnishings, accessories, and clothing are all made from Harris Tweed.

Jewelry crafted by hand: The Isle of Harris is home to talented adornments producers who make flawless pieces roused by the island's normal excellence. These artisans create one-of-a-kind pieces of jewelry by utilizing precious metals like gold and silver. The designs frequently incorporate local gemstones, shells, and nautical themes. Harris' handcrafted jewelry, which ranges from delicate necklaces to intricate earrings, reflects the island's distinctive character.

Ceramic and Pottery: Neighborhood potters and clay specialists feature their craftsmanship through perfectly handmade stoneware and pottery. These artists use traditional techniques to create one-of-a-kind works that are inspired by the rugged seascapes and landscapes of the Isle of Harris. From utilitarian silverware to embellishing figures, their work catches the pith of the island's regular components and surfaces.

Artworks and Photography: Artists and photographers have long used the breathtaking beauty of the Isle of Harris as a source of inspiration. Through their paintings and photographs, numerous island artists capture the island's stunning landscapes, vibrant wildlife, and dramatic seascapes. Whether it's a reasonable depiction or a theoretical translation, these fine arts offer a brief look into the exceptional and steadily changing person of the island.

Carving and woodworking: On the Isle of Harris, skilled carvers and woodworkers use local timber to create intricate pieces. From hand-cut figures and multifaceted furniture to wooden dishes and utensils, their craftsmanship mirrors a profound appreciation for the normal assets of the island. The designs of many of these artisans are influenced by the local wildlife, Celtic motifs, and maritime heritage.

On the Isle of Harris, visitors can visit local craft studios, galleries, and workshops to see these artisans at work and buy one-of-a-kind items directly from the artisans. The island's obligation to safeguarding conventional art procedures and supporting neighborhood craftsmans guarantees that the lively legacy of Harris is praised and esteemed through these excellent specialties and works of art.

Festivals and Events

The Outer Hebrides of Scotland's Isle of Harris is known for its stunning natural beauty, rugged landscapes, and extensive cultural heritage. Over time, the island has different celebrations and occasions that praise its interesting practices, music, artworks, and history. On the Isle of Harris, the following notable festivals and events are held:

Festival at Harris Mountain: An annual celebration of the island's magnificent mountains and landscapes is the Harris Mountain Festival. It offers a scope of exercises, for example, directed strolls, climbs, mountain trekking, untamed life spotting, and photography studios. While learning about the island's geology, flora, and fauna, participants can explore its rugged terrain.

Harris Tweed Ride: The Harris Tweed Ride is a cycling occasion that joins the island's affection for cycling and its renowned Harris Tweed texture. Cycle participants through Harris' stunning landscapes in traditional tweed attire, showcasing the island's beauty. The event emphasizes the significance of Harris Tweed as a local industry while also promoting sustainable travel and bicycle use.

Celtic Festival on the Hebrides: Although not selective to the Isle of Harris, the Hebridean Celtic Celebration is a significant occasion in the External Hebrides and draws in guests from everywhere. The festival, which is held in Stornoway on the Isle of Lewis, showcases the best of Scottish and international talent with a vibrant lineup of traditional and contemporary music artists. It's a fantastic chance to experience the region's cultural heritage and traditional music.

Harris Expressions Celebration: The Harris Expressions Celebration is a yearly festival of artistic expression and specialties of the island. For a week, it brings together local musicians, performers, artists, and artisans. Exhibitions, workshops, live performances, and demonstrations showcasing a variety of artistic fields, such as painting, sculpture, pottery, weaving, and traditional music, are available to visitors.

Ceilidhs and Conventional Music Meetings: On the Isle of Harris, pubs, community halls, and other venues host regular ceilidhs (traditional Scottish social gatherings with music and dancing) and traditional music sessions throughout the year. These occasions give an energetic and credible experience of Scottish music and culture, frequently including gifted neighborhood performers playing conventional instruments like fiddles, bagpipes, and accordions.

Harris Refinery Occasions: The Isle of Harris is home to the eminent Harris Refinery, where the amazingly popular Isle of Harris Gin is created. Events like gin tastings, workshops, and tours are held at the distillery from time to time to provide insight into the gin-making process and the island's extensive distilling history. It's a valuable chance to find out about the craftsmanship behind this commended soul and partake in the flavors exceptional to the Isle of Harris.

It is always recommended to check the official websites or the local tourist information centers for the most up-to-date information on festivals and events happening on the Isle of Harris. Please keep in mind that event schedules and availability may change from year to year.

Tourist Information Center

The rugged landscapes, stunning beaches, and rich cultural heritage of the Isle of Harris, in the Outer Hebrides of Scotland, make it a stunningly beautiful island. The Isle of Harris has a well-equipped Tourist Information Center that provides helpful information and resources to help you have a better time on the island.

In order to get the most out of their time on the Isle of Harris, visitors can find information, direction, and suggestions at the Tourist Information Center, which serves as a knowledge hub. The center is a great place to start your adventures, whether you're interested in nature, history, or just the region's hidden treasures.

At the Traveler Data Center, you'll find a well disposed and proficient staff prepared to help you with a great many administrations. Brochures, maps, and leaflets with comprehensive information about the island's attractions, lodging options, transportation, and upcoming events are available from them. The staff individuals are knowledgeable in the island's set of experiences, geology, and culture, and are consistently anxious to share their skill and suggestions.

In addition to information, the center may provide amenities like accessible restrooms, free Wi-Fi, and a cozy seating area where you can unwind, plan your itinerary, or take a break from exploring. You might also find a small souvenir shop inside the center, where you can get books, maps, locally made crafts, and other mementos to remember your trip.

On the Isle of Harris, there are a wide range of activities to choose from, and the Tourist Information Center can guide you through them.

The staff at the center can suggest itineraries that are tailored to your interests and assist you in booking tours, excursions, or accommodations in accordance, such as hiking along the rugged coastline and discovering ancient ruins, experiencing the world-renowned Harris Tweed industry, and enjoying fresh seafood delicacies.

In addition, the center might host special events, workshops, or exhibitions to highlight the island's distinctive culture, arts, and traditions. This could incorporate exhibitions of conventional specialties like winding around Harris Tweed or displaying nearby performers and artists, allowing guests an opportunity to drench themselves in the island's lively legacy.

Whether you're a first-time guest or getting back to the Isle of Harris, the Vacationer Data Center is an important asset that can improve your excursion. It ensures that you have access to the most recent and accurate information, allowing you to create priceless memories as you discover this extraordinary island's captivating history and enchanting landscapes.

Chapter Three

Top Attractions

The following are ten top attractions on the Isle of Harris, an island situated in the External Hebrides of Scotland:

Beach Luskentyre: Luskentyre Beach is frequently cited as one of the world's most beautiful beaches due to its pristine white sands and turquoise waters.

Standing Stones in Callanish: This old stone circle traces all the way back to around 3000 BC and is a significant archeological site. With its intriguing stone formations, it conveys a sense of mystery and history.

Distillery on the Isle of Harris Visit the Isle of Harris Distillery to learn more about how Harris Gin, a spirit made locally that has island-specific flavors, is made. Take a tour of the distillery and take in the stunning views.

Seilebost Ocean side: Seilebost, another stunning beach on the island, has golden sand, expansive views of the Atlantic Ocean, and a tranquil atmosphere.

Huisinis Ocean side: Huisinis Beach is a tranquil haven on the west coast of Harris. Its remote location provides stunning views and a peaceful haven.

Rodel's St. Clement's Church: Stained glass windows and intricate carvings adorn this medieval church. A fine example of Scottish Gothic architecture can be found here.

The Shop for Harris Tweed: Investigate the extraordinary legacy of Harris Tweed, a conventional hand woven texture. Purchase authentic tweed goods and learn about the weaving process at the Harris Tweed Shop.

Beach Scarista: Scarista Beach is renowned for its wild beauty against the dramatic backdrop of hills and mountains. It's a phenomenal spot for strolls, picnics, and partaking in the tough beachfront scene.

Leverburgh: A little town on the southern tip of Harris, Leverburgh offers dazzling perspectives on the Sound of Harris. You can go on boat outings from here to investigate the encompassing islands.

Observation of Eagles in North Harris: The North Harris Eagle Observatory, which is close to Tarbert, lets you see golden eagles and other birds in their natural environment. Your experience will be enhanced by the knowledgeable staff and guided walks.

The natural beauty, historical significance, and cultural heritage of the Isle of Harris are all showcased by these attractions, making it a truly captivating location to explore.

Outdoor Activities

In the Outer Hebrides of Scotland, the Isle of Harris has a stunning natural landscape and a wide variety of outdoor activities for tourists to enjoy. This island paradise is a haven for outdoor enthusiasts thanks to its dramatic mountains, crystal-clear lochs, rugged coastlines, and golden beaches. On the Isle of Harris, you can participate in the following exciting outdoor activities:

Walking and Hiking :There are scenic walking and hiking trails on the Isle of Harris for people of all fitness levels. While taking in the breathtaking views of the Atlantic Ocean, take in the rocky hillsides, moorlands, and coastal paths. The well known Harris Slopes, for example, the Clisham and the North Harris slopes, offer testing climbs and compensating scenes.

Watersports and the Beach: The island is famous for its white-sand beaches, such as Scarista Beach, Seilebost Beach, and Luskentyre Beach. These unspoiled spots give an ideal background to sunbathing, picnicking, and comfortable strolls along the shore. Moreover, the reasonable waters around Harris are great for different water sports like kayaking, paddleboarding, and surfing.

Observing Wildlife: The Isle of Harris is home to a different exhibit of natural life. Look out for brilliant falcons taking off through the skies, red deer meandering the slopes, and seals relaxing on the rough shores. Along the coastline, you might even come across otters, whales, or dolphins if you're lucky. The unspoiled, remote environment of the island makes it a great place to connect with nature and see these magnificent creatures in their natural environment.

Angling and fishing: The Isle of Harris is a fishing lovers' paradise thanks to its numerous lochs, rivers, and coastal waters. Whether you favor freshwater or saltwater fishing, you'll track down a lot of chances to project your line and take a stab. Fishers can target salmon, trout, and ocean fish, and there are neighborhood fishing guides accessible to give tips and help.

Cycling: A fantastic way to appreciate the island's natural beauty is to tour it on two wheels. The tranquil streets and tourist detours make it an optimal objective for cyclists, everything being equal. There are rides for everyone, from easy rides along the coast to more difficult rides through the interior's hills. On the island, visitors can rent bikes to easily get to and enjoy the great outdoors.

Boat Outings and Island Jumping: Go on a boat outing or leave on an island-bouncing experience to investigate the encompassing islands and experience the marine marvels of the External Hebrides. The historic town of Stornoway and the well-known Callanish Standing Stones can be found on the neighboring Isle of Lewis. You can also travel further to St. Kilda, a UNESCO World Heritage Site, or the far-flung Flannan Isles.

Always keep an eye on the weather and plan your outdoor activities accordingly. The Isle of Harris offers a surprising setting for a large number of outside pursuits, making it an ideal objective for nature darlings and travelers looking for a remarkable involvement with the core of Scotland's shocking scene.

Nature Tour

The rugged landscapes, pristine beaches, and abundance of wildlife on the Isle of Harris, which is in the Outer Hebrides of Scotland, make it a captivating destination. A nature visit in the Isle of Harris offers a striking open door to investigate the island's regular marvels, drench yourself in its serene climate, and find the different widely varied vegetation that call this spot home.

Prepare to be captivated by the dramatic scenery that unfolds before you as you begin your nature tour. The island is made up of mountains, moorlands, and coastal cliffs that are all covered in a colorful tapestry. Whether you're an eager climber, birdwatcher, or basically a nature lover, the Isle of Harris offers an overflow of exercises and sights to enjoy.

One of the most famous highlights of the island is its shocking sea shores. The white sands of Luskentyre, Scarista, and Seilebost are well-known for their unbroken stretches of sand and turquoise waters. Go for a relaxed walk along the coastline, take in the new ocean air, and relish the peacefulness of these disconnected safe houses. You might even see dolphins gracefully gliding through the water or seals basking on the rocks.

You'll come across rugged terrain with high mountains and vast moorlands if you go further inland. Lace up your hiking boots and explore the verdant expanses of the North Harris Hills or the breathtaking Clisham Hills, the Outer Hebrides' highest peak. As you climb, you'll be compensated with all encompassing vistas that exhibit the island's untamed excellence and proposition looks at adjoining islands.

With its diverse population of feathered residents, the Isle of Harris is a haven for birdwatchers. If you go out into the wild with binoculars handy, you might be able to see majestic golden eagles soaring overhead or red-throated divers gracefully gliding across lochs. Puffins, razorbills, and guillemots are just a few of the seabirds that nest on the island's coastal cliffs, which make for an unforgettable avian sight.

On nature tours on the Isle of Harris, you can also learn about the island's extensive cultural history. Explore traditional crofting villages, where locals continue to engage in traditional farming practices, or visit ancient sites like the Standing Stones of Callanish, a neolithic stone circle that has stood for more than 5,000 years. Draw in with the amicable islanders, find out about their lifestyle, and find the profound association they share with the land and ocean.

To take advantage of your temperament visit, consider drawing in the administrations of experienced neighborhood guides who have top to bottom information on the island's regular history, geography, and untamed life. They can offer bits of knowledge into the island's unexpected, yet invaluable treasures, guide you to the best vantage points for untamed life spotting, and guarantee that you have a safe and enhancing experience.

A nature tour on the Isle of Harris promises an unforgettable journey, whether you're looking for peace and quiet or an adventure in wild landscapes. Explore the island's diverse ecosystems, take in its pristine beauty, and revel in the wonders of this remote paradise. The Isle of Harris is a true haven where nature reigns supreme, providing both a chance to reconnect with the primordial forces that shape our planet and a respite from the demands of modern life.

Setting Budget

When you go to Scotland's Isle of Harris, setting a budget can help you get the most out of your trip and have an unforgettable time without breaking the bank. You can make a budget for your time on the Isle of Harris by following these steps:

Decide your general excursion spending plan: Start by concluding the amount you can bear to spend on your whole excursion to the Isle of Harris. Take into account costs associated with transportation, lodging, meals, activities, and souvenirs.

Research transportation choices: Consider the various means of transportation, including flights, ferries, or a combination of the two, available to reach the Isle of Harris. Choose the most cost-effective option that meets your needs by comparing prices.

Plan convenience carefully: Investigate different convenience choices on the island, like lodgings, guesthouses, B&Bs, or self-cooking rentals. Look at reviews, compare prices, and think about things like location, amenities, and availability. By preparing some of your own meals, choosing self-catering accommodation can help you save money.

Make a day to day spending plan: Take into account the cost of meals, activities, transportation, and any other additional costs when estimating your daily expenses. Research nearby eateries and food choices to find out about commonplace feast costs. Include the costs of any particular attractions or activities you intend to visit in your daily budget.

Make attractions and activities a priority: On the Isle of Harris, make a list of the things you want to do and see the most. Research their costs and conclude which ones are affordable enough for you. Keep in mind to budget for any costs associated with guided tours, admission, or equipment rentals.

Financial plan for dinners: Plan your meals accordingly because dining out at restaurants can be expensive. If you have access to a kitchen in your lodging, you could save money by cooking some of your own meals instead of going to a more expensive local cafe or restaurant.

Make room for unforeseen costs: It's important to plan your budget in advance, but it's also wise to leave room for unforeseen expenses. Make allowances for various costs, such as mishaps with your transportation, unforeseen activities, or souvenirs you might like to buy.

Be aware of your spending: During your outing, monitor your costs to guarantee you stay affordable enough for you. Record your spending and compare it to your budget by using a notebook, spreadsheet, or budgeting app. If necessary, adjust your expenses to stay on track.

Find low-cost or free activities: The Isle of Harris has numerous scenic landscapes and natural attractions that don't cost a lot of money to enjoy. Investigate climbing trails, visit nearby sea shores, or exploit free occasions or celebrations occurring during your visit.

Be careful with keepsakes: Gifts can add up rapidly, so be specific and pick things that are significant to you. Think about supporting nearby craftsmans and organizations by buying hand tailored or privately created merchandise.

Keep in mind that sticking to a budget doesn't mean sacrificing enjoyment. It just assists you with focusing on your spending and pursuing informed decisions about where to allot your assets. You can have a wonderful time on the Isle of Harris while staying within your budget if you plan ahead and pay attention to your costs.

Chapter Four

Safety Tips

While visiting the Isle of Harris, it's vital to focus on wellbeing to guarantee a wonderful and occurrence free insight. Consider the following safety recommendations:

Weather patterns: The climate on the Isle of Harris can be eccentric, with fast changes. Stay up to date on the weather forecast and be ready for sudden changes. Regardless of the season, bring warm and waterproof layers of clothing with you.

Outdoor pursuits: The island offers amazing scenes and outside exercises like climbing, climbing, and water sports. Assuming that you intend to participate in any open air exercises, ensure you have the essential experience, abilities, and gear. Always let someone know about your plans, especially if you're going somewhere remote or not often visited.

Seaside Wellbeing: The Isle of Harris has staggering shores, yet they can be hazardous in the event that legitimate watchfulness isn't worked out. Focus on cautioning signs, particularly during elevated tides and turbulent climate. The edges of cliffs can be unstable, so keep a safe distance from them. If you don't know much about the area, you might want to ask locals or guides for advice.

Natural life Experiences: The island is home to different natural life species, including seals and seabirds. While noticing natural life, keep a conscious separation and try not to be upset or take care of them. Be especially careful around nesting areas because causing the birds harm could be very bad.

Traffic Safety: Assuming you intend to drive on the Isle of Harris, look into neighborhood traffic rules and guidelines. Be aware that there are places along some roads where there is only one track, so drive with patience and caution. Focus on animals on the streets, as they have the option to proceed in rustic regions.

Water Wellbeing: For novice swimmers, the waters around the Isle of Harris can be cold and difficult. If you decide to swim, make sure you know what to expect, like strong currents and cold temperatures. To safeguard yourself, think about donning a wetsuit or other appropriate gear.

Be respectful of the culture: The Isle of Harris has a rich social legacy, and regarding neighborhood customs and traditions is significant. Draw in with the local area differentially and adhere to any rules given by local people, particularly while visiting consecrated or safeguarded destinations.

Services for Emergencies: Learn the phone numbers for emergency services like the police, ambulance, and coastguard. Keep your mobile phone charged and easily accessible, especially when you're traveling to faraway places where signal strength may be poor.

When you go to the Isle of Harris, keep in mind that your own safety and the safety of others should be your top priority. By being ready, mindful, and deferential of the climate and neighborhood customs, you can have a vital and safe experience on the island.

Health and Medical Services

The stunning Isle of Harris can be found in Scotland's Outer Hebrides. While it offers stunning scenes and a quiet climate, it is essential to approach dependable medical services administrations to meet the clinical requirements of its inhabitants and guests.

Medical care administrations on the Isle of Harris are given by the Public Wellbeing Administration (NHS) Scotland, which guarantees that the island's populace approaches fundamental clinical consideration. The Isle of Harris Health Centre is the island's primary healthcare facility. It is in Tarbert, the island's main village and administrative center.

The Isle of Harris Wellbeing Center is staffed by a group of general experts (GPs) who give a scope of essential consideration administrations, including normal check-ups, immunizations, and the board of constant circumstances. They assume an essential part locally, offering clinical guidance, diagnosing and treating diseases, and alluding patients to expert administrations or emergency clinics, if vital.

The health center may also have nurses, practice staff, and allied health professionals like pharmacists and physiotherapists who collaborate with the general practitioners to provide comprehensive healthcare services.

Residents of the Isle of Harris may need to travel to Stornoway, the largest town in the Outer Hebrides on the Isle of Lewis, for more specialized medical care. The Western Isles Hospital in Stornoway is a hospital that provides a wider range of medical services, including surgical procedures, diagnostic tests, and emergency care.

Regular ferry services connect the Isle of Harris with Stornoway, making it easy for patients who need more advanced medical care to get there. It is important to note that the Isle of Harris has emergency medical services, such as ambulances, to ensure prompt response to emergencies.

On the Isle of Harris, there may be one or two local pharmacies that offer both over-the-counter and prescription medications. Nonetheless, the scope of administrations and accessibility of drugs might be more restricted contrasted with bigger towns or urban areas.

It is essential to keep in mind that, like healthcare systems in other remote areas, the Isle of Harris's geographical location and small population may present obstacles. However, the healthcare professionals strive to ensure the community's wellbeing and provide high-quality care.

Prior to visiting or dwelling on the Isle of Harris, it is prescribed to have suitable health care coverage inclusion to address any unexpected clinical necessities. In addition, the most up-to-date information on the island's healthcare services and facilities can be found on the NHS Scotland website or from healthcare providers.

Overall, despite the fact that the Isle of Harris may have fewer healthcare resources than urban areas, the island's healthcare providers and facilities work hard to ensure the health and wellbeing of the island's residents and visitors.

Safety and Emergency contacts

The stunning landscapes, rugged coastlines, and vibrant communities of the Isle of Harris, which is in the Outer Hebrides of Scotland, have earned it a reputation. Even though it's a relatively safe place to go, you should always put your safety first and be ready for anything that might happen. The Isle of Harris' emergency contacts and safety information are as follows:

Services for Emergencies:

To contact the emergency services in the event of an emergency, dial 999 or 112 from any phone. Depending on the circumstances, these numbers will connect you to the fire department, ambulance, or police department.

Services for the sick:

The Isle of Harris has a couple of clinical offices to take special care of inhabitants and guests. The Western Isles Hospital in Stornoway, on the Isle of Lewis, is the main medical facility. It offers emergency care among other medical services. For non-crisis clinical issues, you can visit the Harris and Scalpay People group Medical clinic in Tarbert, which gives essential **medical services administrations.**

Western Isles Medical clinic (Stornoway):

Address: Macaulay Street, Stornoway, Isle of Lewis, HS1 2AF

Contact: Harris and Scalpay Community Hospital (Tarbert): +44 (0)1851 704704

Address: Tarbert, Isle of Harris, Harris and Scalpay Community Hospital, HS3 3BG +44 (0)1859 502131 Maritime and **Coastguard Emergencies:**

The Coastguard should be contacted in case of maritime emergencies due to the stunning coastline of the Isle of Harris. They are in charge of the coast-based search and rescue operations.

Coast Guard: In an emergency

Dial 999 or 112 and request the Coastguard

Police Administrations:

Police Scotland is the local police department on the Isle of Harris. They are answerable for keeping up with the rule of law on the island.

Police (Non-crisis):

Mountain Rescue: For non-emergency police assistance, dial 101.

On the off chance that you're wanting to investigate the rocky districts of the Isle of Harris and wind up needing help, the Mountain Salvage group can help. They spend significant time in salvages in tough landscapes and distant regions.

Emergency Mountain Rescue:

Make a request for Mountain Rescue Travel Safety by dialing 999 or 112:

While investigating the Isle of Harris, it's fundamental to avoid potential risk to guarantee your wellbeing. Be aware of the accompanying:

At popular tourist destinations, adhere to any safety instructions or signs.

To avoid accidents and harm to fragile ecosystems, stay on marked paths and trails.

Before engaging in outdoor activities, especially in remote areas, check the weather.

Include a map or GPS device, food, water, and appropriate clothing in your bag of essentials.

If you're going somewhere off the beaten path, be sure to tell someone about your travel plans and the estimated time of your return.

Researching and getting ready for your trip to the Isle of Harris in advance is always a good idea. To ensure a safe and enjoyable trip, familiarize yourself with local safety regulations and guidelines.

Currency and Exchange

Isle of Harris, situated in the External Hebrides of Scotland, is known for its stunning scenes, tough shores, and rich social legacy. Isle of

Harris, a remote and distinct island, uses the currency of the United Kingdom. The authority money utilized on the island, as in the remainder of Scotland and the UK, is the British Pound sterling (£).

The Isle of Harris currency exchange follows the same rules as the rest of the UK. Guests to the island will track down different choices for trading their money into English Pounds. Here are a few normal techniques for money trade:

Banks: The most secure and dependable places to exchange currency are banks. The Bank of Scotland is the main bank on the Isle of Harris, and it has a branch in the town of Tarbert. Guests can visit the bank during their opening times to trade their cash. Before making plans to visit, it's best to check the bank's hours of operation.

ATMs: On the Isle of Harris, including the populated town of Tarbert and other areas, there are ATMs (automated teller machines). These ATMs give out British Pounds and accept major credit and debit cards. However, it is always a good idea to tell your bank about your plans to travel so that they can make sure your cards work properly while you're away and see whether there are extra charges

Money Trade Workplaces: There may be some local businesses that provide currency exchange services, despite the fact that there are fewer currency exchange offices on the Isle of Harris than in larger cities. These workplaces typically charge a commission or expense for their administrations, and the trade rates may not be pretty much as good as those presented by banks. Before choosing this option, it's best to compare rates and fees.

Cards for Prepaid Travel: Visitors to the Isle of Harris can take advantage of the convenience of prepaid travel cards. You can get a fixed exchange rate by loading your preferred currency onto these cards prior to your trip. Travel cards can be used at ATMs and merchants that accept card payments to make purchases. However, it is essential to confirm the card's widespread acceptance on the island and inquire about any fees.

It is recommended to consider the potential transaction fees, commissions, and exchange rates when exchanging currency on the Isle of Harris. For convenience and in case of emergency, it's also a good idea to carry a variety of payment options, like cash and credit cards.

Likewise with any movement objective, it merits investigating the ongoing trade rates and seeing any guidelines or restrictions in regards to money trade before your visit to the Isle of Harris. When it comes to managing your finances on the island, this will help ensure that everything runs smoothly and without any problems.

Chapter Five

Food and Drinks

The Outer Hebrides of Scotland's Isle of Harris is renowned for its vibrant culture, rugged coastlines, and stunning landscapes. In addition to that, it is a spot where you can savor delectable beverages and food that pay homage to the island's distinctive character and abundant natural resources. How about we investigate the culinary joys of the Isle of Harris.

Seafood:

Seafood takes center stage on the Isle of Harris because the island is surrounded by abundant North Atlantic waters. You can relish newly got langoustines, scallops, crab, lobster, and mussels, ready in different heavenly ways. The flavors of the sea will make you want more, whether you order a seafood platter at a local restaurant or have a casual picnic with freshly shucked oysters at the beach.

Harris Gin:

The Isle of Harris is eminent for its privately delivered gin, suitably named Harris Gin. Made with botanicals obtained from the island's scene, including sugar kelp reaped from the sea, this soul catches the quintessence of Harris. The gin has a flavor profile that is both complex and harmonious, with citrus, floral, and sea-freshness notes. A visit to the Isle of Harris is incomplete without examining this interesting and grant winning gin.

Tea: Harris Tweed:

Enjoy a cup of Harris Tweed Tea for a taste of tradition. This specialty tea is a blend of black teas that evoke warmth and comfort, and it was named after the island's famous tweed fabric. Experience a truly authentic island custom by sipping on a steaming cup while munching on locally baked treats like shortbread or scones.

Whisky from the Hebrides:

It should come as no surprise that the Isle of Harris is home to some exceptional distilleries, which will please whisky connoisseurs. You can try a variety of Hebridean whiskies that are made on neighboring islands while the island's own whisky is still in the process of maturing. These whiskies frequently show unmistakable flavors affected by the sea environment, peat, and the one of a kind person of the encompassing scene.

Local Products:

The Isle of Harris is likewise an optimal spot to enjoy new, privately developed produce. The island's fertile land and traditional farming methods produce high-quality ingredients, such as organic herbs, vegetables, and succulent lamb and beef. Nearby ranchers' business sectors and shops offer a variety of occasional natural products, vegetables, cheeses, and meats that mirror the island's rich rural legacy.

Food from Scotland's past:

While the Isle of Harris has its own culinary character, you can likewise track down customary Scottish dishes on the island. Appreciate good top picks like haggis, dark pudding, and Cullen skink — a rich and smooth soup made with smoked haddock. These dishes often use ingredients that are sourced locally, giving you a taste of Scotland's rich culinary history.

Whether you're a fish sweetheart, a gin epicurean, or a pilgrim of customary flavors, the Isle of Harris offers a different scope of food and beverages that commend the island's regular environmental elements and social legacy. Drench yourself in the culinary pleasures of this lovely island and let your taste buds leave on a really significant excursion.

Traditional and Scottish Cuisine

The Isle of Harris, located in the Outer Hebrides of Scotland, is renowned for its stunning landscapes and rich cultural heritage. The island offers a unique culinary experience that combines traditional Scottish cuisine with local ingredients and flavors. Let's explore the traditional and Scottish cuisine of the Isle of Harris.

Traditional Cuisine:

The traditional cuisine of the Isle of Harris reflects its history and the reliance on local resources. Due to its coastal location, seafood plays a significant role in the island's traditional dishes. Some popular traditional dishes include:

Smoked Salmon: The island's pristine waters are home to an abundance of salmon, which is often smoked using traditional methods. The smoky and rich flavors make it a sought-after delicacy.

Stornoway Black Pudding: Stornoway, a nearby town on the Isle of Lewis, produces renowned black pudding. Made from a combination of oats, pork, onions, and spices, it has a distinct flavor and is considered a staple breakfast item.

Haggis: Though haggis is a traditional Scottish dish, it can also be found on the Isle of Harris. This savory pudding is made with sheep's offal, oats, onions, and spices, traditionally encased in a sheep's stomach. It is usually served with neeps (turnips) and tatties (potatoes).

Scottish Cuisine:

Scottish cuisine has a strong presence on the Isle of Harris, with local establishments embracing traditional Scottish recipes. Some Scottish dishes you can find on the island include:

Cullen Skink: A hearty soup originating from the town of Cullen in Scotland, Cullen Skink is a creamy fish soup made with smoked haddock, potatoes, onions, and milk. It is a warming and flavorsome dish, perfect for colder days.

Scotch Broth: This traditional Scottish soup is made with lamb or mutton, barley, and an assortment of vegetables such as carrots, leeks, and turnips. It is a nourishing and filling dish, often enjoyed during the winter months.

Cranachan: A delightful Scottish dessert, cranachan is made by layering toasted oats, raspberries, honey, and whipped cream. Sometimes whisky is added to give it an extra kick.

Local Ingredients:

The Isle of Harris boasts an array of fresh, local ingredients that are incorporated into both traditional and Scottish dishes. Some of the local ingredients that feature prominently in the cuisine include:

Seafood: Being an island, the Isle of Harris offers an abundance of seafood such as lobster, crab, scallops, and mussels. These delicacies are often prepared simply to let the natural flavors shine through.

Lamb: The island's lush pastures provide excellent grazing for sheep, resulting in high-quality lamb. The tender and flavorsome meat is used in various dishes, including stews and roasts.

Barley: Barley, a staple crop on the island, is used in soups, stews, and traditional Scottish dishes like Scotch broth and barley bannocks.

Berries: The island is home to an assortment of wild berries, including raspberries, blackberries, and blueberries. These berries are often used in desserts, jams, and sauces.

Visiting the Isle of Harris offers an opportunity to indulge in a unique culinary experience that combines traditional Scottish recipes with the island's local ingredients. Whether you're savoring the flavors of freshly caught seafood or enjoying a comforting bowl of Cullen Skink, the cuisine of the Isle of Harris will delight your taste buds and leave you with a lasting impression of this beautiful Scottish island.

Best Restaurants and Bars

The Isle of Harris, situated in the External Hebrides of Scotland, is known for its dazzling scenes, unblemished sea shores, and rich Gaelic legacy. While it very well might be a remote and inadequately populated island, it offers a couple of incredible eating and drinking foundations that grandstand the best of neighborhood produce and flavors. On the Isle of Harris, some of the best restaurants and bars are as follows:

Bistro North Harbour: Arranged in the pleasant town of Scalpay, the North Harbor Bistro offers a great eating experience with all encompassing perspectives on the Harris slopes and the Scalpay Scaffold. The menu centers around privately obtained fish and conventional Scottish dishes, ready with an imaginative turn. Each dish, from hand-dived langoustines to fresh scallops, is beautifully presented and packed with flavor.

The restaurant in Anchorage: The Anchorage Restaurant, which is in Leverburgh, is known for its excellent food and warm service. The menu joins current Scottish food with worldwide impacts, highlighting dishes made with privately obtained fixings, for example, Hebridean sheep and Harris Gin-injected salmon. It is a popular choice for both tourists and locals due to the welcoming atmosphere and helpful staff.

Restaurant at Hebrides Hotel: The Hotel Hebrides has a stylish restaurant that serves the finest island produce and is located in Tarbert, the main village on the Isle of Harris. The menu includes different dishes, including newly got fish, delicious steaks, and vegan choices. This restaurant offers a charming setting for a memorable dining experience with its modern decor and harbor views.

Restaurant at Amhuinnsuidhe Castle: For a really exceptional feasting experience, consider visiting the Amhuinnsuidhe Palace Eatery. This elegant restaurant on the Isle of Harris is inside a historic castle. It has a refined menu that is based on local ingredients and traditional Scottish recipes. With its excellent environmental factors and mindful help, feasting at Amhuinnsuidhe Palace is a treat for both the sense of taste and the faculties.

Bar MacLeod: In the event that you're searching for a comfortable spot to partake in a beverage and absorb the island climate, MacLeod's Bar in Tarbert is a well known decision. A wide variety of Scottish whiskies, local ales, and refreshing cocktails are available at this traditional pub. With unrecorded music exhibitions and a cordial vibe, it's an optimal spot to loosen up and blend with local people and individual voyagers.

The Harris Inn Bar: This bar in the Harris Hotel offers a casual setting for a drink after a day of island exploration. The bar offers a broad determination of spirits, including neighborhood gins and malt whiskies, alongside a scope of wines and brews. With its open to seating and inviting environment, it's an incredible spot to loosen up and enjoy the kinds of the district.

Although there are only a few restaurants and bars on the Isle of Harris, these establishments take great pride in providing exceptional service, warm hospitality, and a genuine taste of the island's culinary delights. Whether you're looking for new fish, customary Scottish dishes, or a fine determination of beverages, these scenes on the Isle of Harris will leave you fulfilled and anxious to investigate a greater amount of the island's normal magnificence.

Shopping and Nightlife

In the Outer Hebrides of Scotland, the Isle of Harris is known for its stunning natural landscapes, pristine beaches, and extensive

Gaelic heritage. The island may be known for its scenic beauty, but it also offers visitors unique shopping experiences and a lively nightlife.

When you go shopping on the Isle of Harris, you can learn about exquisite local art and craftsmanship. One of the most well known attractions is the Harris Tweed, an extravagant hand woven texture that has been created on the island for quite a long time. You can investigate the Harris Tweed shops and studios, where you'll find a large number of items produced using this special material, including dress, embellishments, and home decorations. It's a great way to give back to the community and take home a piece of Harris's history.

In addition to Harris Tweed, other local artisans and craftsmen offer a variety of products that showcase their skills. Beautifully crafted jewelry, pottery, paintings, and sculptures, all of which reflect the island's distinctive character and artistic traditions, can be found in galleries and boutiques. These foundations frequently give a potential chance to meet the craftsmen, find out about their innovative strategies, and gain exceptional pieces.

The Isle of Harris has a lively nightlife scene as the day turns to night. The island lacks large-scale entertainment venues or bustling clubs, but its unique atmosphere and cozy establishments make up for it. Visitors and locals alike congregate in the area's pubs and bars to unwind, listen to live music, and share tales over a pint of locally brewed ale.

Traditional music sessions are frequently held in the island's pubs, where you can anticipate a warm and friendly welcome. Talented local musicians perform traditional Scottish songs in a magical setting that immerses you in the region's rich cultural heritage. Impromptu ceilidh dances are common, and both locals and visitors take part in the lively celebrations.

The Isle of Harris offers a peaceful and tranquil nightlife experience beyond the pubs. The island is a haven for stargazers because it has little light pollution. Due to the dominance of the dark skies, you can enjoy breathtaking views of the starry sky on clear nights. The Isle of Harris offers an exceptional opportunity to marvel at the wonders of the universe, whether you choose to explore the night sky on your own or take part in a guided tour of the constellations.

Overall, the Isle of Harris's nightlife offers a mix of lively pubs, traditional music sessions, and the chance to look at the stars, and shopping there lets you discover one-of-a-kind local craftsmanship. Whether you're looking to bring back a piece of the island's legacy or submerge yourself in its dynamic culture, Harris gives an important and captivating experience for guests.

Chapter Six

Travel Tips

The Isle of Harris can be visited with the following travel tips:

Make a visit plan: The Outer Hebrides, specifically the Isle of Harris, are in Scotland. To get the most out of your time on the island, conduct research and make advance plans for your trip. Consider the length of your visit, the best opportunity to visit, and the exercises you might want to encounter.

How to get there: The ferry is the most common means of getting to the Isle of Harris. You can get a ship from Uig on the Isle of Skye to Tarbert, which is the fundamental port on Harris. On the other hand, you can fly into Stornoway on the Isle of Lewis and afterward drive or take a transport to Harris.

Car leasing: Having a vehicle is energetically suggested on Harris as it permits you to investigate the island at your own speed. In order to guarantee availability, book your rental car in advance, particularly during peak tourist season. Make sure to drive on the left half of the street in Scotland.

Accommodation: There are different choices for convenience on the Isle of Harris, including lodgings, overnight boarding houses, self-catering bungalows, and campgrounds. It's prudent to book your convenience ahead of time, particularly assuming that you're visiting throughout the late spring months.

Climate and dress: The climate on the Isle of Harris can be inconsistent, so it's critical to pack layers and be ready for various circumstances. Indeed, even in the late spring, it tends to be blustery and crisp, so bring a waterproof coat, comfortable dress, and strong shoes for open air exercises.

Outdoor pursuits: The stunning landscapes and outdoor activities that can be found on the Isle of Harris are well-known. Explore the beautiful beaches with their white sand and turquoise waters, like Scarista and Luskentyre, don't miss out. Climbing devotees can partake in the difficult territory of the Harris Slopes, including Clisham, the most elevated top in the External Hebrides.

Birding and wildlife watching: The island is home to a different scope of natural life, including seals, otters, falcons, and seabirds. Look out for these entrancing animals during your visit. Additionally, there are boat tours available for watching whales and dolphins.

Nearby culture: Find opportunity to drench yourself in the neighborhood culture of Harris. Learn about the old-fashioned methods of weaving at the Harris Tweed shops. Investigate the noteworthy locales, like the well known standing stones of Callanish on the adjoining Isle of Lewis.

Nearby food: Try not to pass up on the opportunity to test nearby indulgences, like newly gotten fish, including scallops and langoustines. At one of the local pubs, you can sample traditional Scottish dishes like haggis and a glass of whisky.

Respect the natural world: The Isle of Harris is known for its flawless and untainted scenes. Assist with protecting its normal excellence by being capable and deferential of the climate. Follow assigned ways, discard squander appropriately, and comply with any neighborhood rules or limitations.

Keep in mind, these tips are intended to upgrade your experience on the Isle of Harris. Make memories that will last a lifetime on this stunning Scottish island!

Do's and Don't For Tourists

The Isle of Harris is important for the bigger Isle of Harris and Isle of Lewis, which are situated in the External Hebrides of Scotland. It's critical to keep in mind that some rules and regulations might have changed. For the most up-to-date information, it is always recommended to consult the most recent official sources, such as local tourism websites or authorities. For tourists visiting the Isle of Harris, the following are some general guidelines:

Do's

Take in the breathtaking natural beauty: The Isle of Harris is known for its stunning scenery, which includes pristine turquoise waters, rugged mountains, and white sand beaches. The island's natural wonders are encouraged to be discovered and appreciated by tourists.

Visit verifiable and social destinations: The island is wealthy in history and culture. Guests can investigate old standing stones, customary covered bungalows, and find out about the Gaelic legacy of the locale. St. Clement's Church in Rodel and the renowned Callanish Standing Stones are two well-known tourist attractions.

Participate in outside exercises: The Isle of Harris offers great open doors for outside pursuits. Travelers can observe the diverse flora and fauna by hiking, fishing, birdwatching, cycling, kayaking, or participating in wildlife tours.

Support neighborhood organizations: The island has a thriving community with shops, restaurants, and artisans. Sightseers are urged to help the nearby economy by buying privately made creations, appreciating conventional food and drink, and remaining in facilities given by neighborhood foundations.

Don't

Upset untamed life or their territories: Regarding the common habitat and untamed life on the Isle of Harris is significant. Try not to be upset or take care of wild creatures, and notice them from a protected distance. Also, take care not to harm or upset delicate natural surroundings like hills or settling regions.

Littering: Visitors should either use the designated bins or take their trash with them so that they do not leave any litter behind. Keeping the island clean aides safeguard its excellence and safeguards the nearby untamed life.

Private property intruder: Even though Scotland has rights to public access, it's important to respect private property and get permission before entering areas that aren't marked as public spaces. Continuously adhere to any posted signs or directions with respect to get to and guarantee that you are not encroaching upon anybody's security.

disregarding the traditions and customs of the area: Traditional practices and a strong sense of community characterize the Isle of Harris. Respect for local customs, traditions, and ways of life is essential. For instance, if visiting a nearby church or partaking in a widespread development, dress unobtrusively and adhere to any rules or directions gave.

Before making plans for a trip to the Isle of Harris, it is best to consult the most recent official sources or get in touch with local authorities or tourism organizations to get the most up-to-date information. These guidelines are meant to be general information.

Conclusion

Taking everything into account, the Isle of Harris is a charming and spellbinding island that exhibits the absolute best of Scotland's normal excellence. With its tough scenes, unblemished sea shores, and turquoise waters, an objective has an enduring impact on all who visit.

All through its rich history, the Isle of Harris has stayed consistent with its practices and social legacy. The island's occupants, known for their glow and cordiality, have figured out how to safeguard their lifestyle while embracing current impacts. The island is full of one-of-a-kind customs, including the local Gaelic language and the world-famous Harris Tweed industry.

On the Isle of Harris, nature lovers will find paradise. There is a sense of tranquility and awe-inspiring beauty that permeates the island, whether you are strolling along the untouched shores or exploring the dramatic cliffs and mountains that dominate the landscape. From the notable Luskentyre Ocean side to the rough pinnacles of the Harris Slopes, each corner offers another experience ready to be found.

Past its regular ponders, the Isle of Harris additionally gives amazing open doors to outside exercises like climbing, fishing, and birdwatching. It is where one can submerge themselves in the untamed wild and reconnect with the crude force of nature.

Additionally, the island's close-knit community and commitment to sustainable tourism guarantee a meaningful and authentic experience for visitors. From charming guest houses to artisanal shops, the island's local businesses provide opportunities to support the local economy and provide a glimpse into the island's way of life.

The Isle of Harris is essentially a destination that exemplifies the rugged beauty, rich heritage, and warm hospitality of Scotland. This remarkable island offers a truly unforgettable experience, whether you're looking for solace in the natural world, want to delve into the cultural fabric of the island, or just want to enjoy the slower pace of life. Visitors can appreciate the simplest pleasures and find solace in the wild wilderness at this location, where time seems to stand still. The Isle of Harris is a treasure trove that is waiting to be discovered and treasured by all who visit its shores.

Printed in Great Britain
by Amazon